New Vanguard • 131

US Field Artillery
of World War II

Steven J Zaloga • Illustrated by Brian Delf

First published in Great Britain in 2007 by Osprey Publishing,
Midland House, West Way, Botley, Oxford OX2 0PH, UK
44-02 23rd St, Suite 219, Long Island City, NY 11101, USA
Email: info@ospreypublishing.com

Transferred to digital print on demand 2010

First published 2007
3rd impression 2008

Printed and bound by PrintOnDemand-Worldwide.com, Peterborough, UK

A CIP catalog record for this book is available from the British Library

ISBN: 978 1 84603 061 1

Page Layout by Melissa Orrom Swan, Oxford, UK
Index by Alan Thatcher
Origination by PPS Grasmere Ltd, Leeds, UK
Typeset in Helvetica Neue and ITC New Baskerville

Artist's note
Readers may care to note that the original paintings from which the color plates in this book were prepared are available for
private sale. All reproduction copyright whatsoever is retained by the Publishers. All enquiries should be addressed to:

Brian Delf,
7 Burcot Park,
Burcot,
Abingdon,
Oxon,
OX14 3DH
UK

The Publishers regret that they can enter into no correspondence upon this matter.

Glossary

AEF	American Expeditionary Force
ETO	European Theater of Operations
FDC	Fire Direction Center
GMC	Gun Motor Carriage
GPF	*Grande Puissance Filloux*: Filloux High-Power
HMC	Howitzer Motor Carriage
HST	High-Speed Tractor
SPG	Self-Propelled Gun

FOR A CATALOG OF ALL BOOKS PUBLISHED BY
OSPREY MILITARY AND AVIATION PLEASE CONTACT:

Osprey Direct, c/o Random House Distribution Center,
400 Hahn Road, Westminster, MD 21157
Email: uscustomerservice@ospreypublishing.com

Osprey Direct, The Book Service Ltd, Distribution Centre,
Colchester Road, Frating Green, Colchester, Essex, CO7 7DW
Email: customerservice@ospreypublishing.com

www.ospreypublishing.com

US FIELD ARTILLERY
OF WORLD WAR II

INTRODUCTION

Field artillery was the only combat arm of the US Army in World War II in which the United States was clearly the world leader in both technology and tactics. During World War I, the US Army was unprepared for providing its own artillery weapons and therefore was dependent on the supply of French and British artillery. After the Great War, the Army was determined to develop a whole new generation of weapons and so, unlike most European countries, started from scratch in the 1920s and 1930s. In contrast to many European armies, which still relied on various older World War I weapons during the 1939–45 campaigns, the US Army was fully reequipped with new artillery weapons during the campaigns of 1943–45. Apart from the development of a full range of excellent new weapons, the Army also enjoyed the full motorization of its artillery arm, which was a significant advantage in the mobile campaigns of World War II. The new artillery weapons were integrated with an advanced new doctrine that introduced a number of critical innovations, including aerial observation, Fire Direction Centers, and radio communications, which substantially enhanced the firepower of the US field artillery. The focus of this book is on field artillery; weapons such as antitank guns, antiaircraft guns, assault guns, coastal guns, and self-propelled tank destroyers not used by field artillery units are not covered in this volume.

important factor in the effectiveness of US field artillery in World War II was the modernized infrastructure of the artillery battalions. Light aircraft were used for air observation, which increased the effectiveness of the howitzer batteries in long-range engagements. This is a 105mm Howitzer M1A1 on Carriage M2 from one of the battalions of the 29th Division during training exercises near Thiseldon in Great Britain in March 1943. (NARA)

THE WORLD WAR I LEGACY

When the United States entered World War I in 1917, it was poorly equipped in modern field artillery. As a result, the American Expeditionary Force (AEF) was heavily dependent on French- and British-manufactured weapons. Rather than develop new indigenous designs, the US Army also turned to the licensed manufacture of these artillery pieces, notably the French 75mm M1897 field gun, the British 18-pdr rechambered for French 75mm ammunition, the French 155mm GPF (*Grande Puissance Filloux*: Filloux High-power) gun, the French Schneider 155mm howitzer, the British 8-in. and 9.2-in. howitzers, and the French 240mm howitzer. A small number of US designs were also manufactured, including a US 75mm Model 1916 field gun rechambered for French 75mm ammunition and the 4.7-in. Model 1906 gun. By the end of the war in November 1918, US-manufactured weapons were beginning to arrive in France; so, for example, the AEF received a total of 1,828 75mm guns from the French and 143 US-manufactured 75mm guns. However, most of the weapons used by US troops during the conflict were of foreign design and manufacture.

The unsatisfactory state of US artillery in World War I prompted the Army Chief of Staff to set up a board to study the problem, headed by Brig Gen William Westervelt. The Westervelt Board, also called the Caliber Board, first met in France in January 1919 and took the opportunity to interview British, French, and Italian artillery specialists, as well as to study German artillery designs. The board submitted its report in May 1919, which concluded that "every item of hardware of war needed improvement." The report of the Westervelt Board had a long-lasting impact on US Army artillery due to its perceptive prescriptions for development. In spite of its sound recommendations, the impact of the Westervelt Board in the short-term was minimal due to the sharp decline in the Army budget after the war. American foreign policy shifted towards isolationism and ardently rejected participation in future European conflicts. The large inventory of artillery weapons built up during World War I seemed more than adequate for the Army's interwar responsibilities.

In light of this situation, the US Army Ordnance Department shifted its focus from the manufacture of artillery weapons to the development of the new weapons recommended by the Westervelt Board. Since funds were limited, the primary focus was on divisional artillery, with less emphasis placed on corps and army artillery. There was substantial debate in the interwar years over the best mix of weapons for the infantry division. The

State of the art in 1918, this Holt Model 55 armored 10-ton tractor is seen towing a Schneider 155mm howitzer during wargames at Pine Camp in upstate New York in the summer of 1935. Some 1,421 of these tractors were delivered by the time of the Armistice, and a total of 2,014 by the end of January 1919. (NARA)

The 75mm Pack Howitzer M1A1 on Carriage M8 was used primarily in light divisions such as the airborne divisions in place of the 105mm howitzer. This howitzer is from the 463d Parachute Field Artillery Battalion supporting the 1st Airborne Tank Force near Hagenau on January 29, 1945, during the repulse of Operation *Nordwind*. (NARA)

primary divisional field artillery weapon in World War I was the 75mm gun, with the French "*soixante-quinze*" 75mm M1897 remaining the most prominent piece in US Army service until the early 1940s. By the late 1930s, the Army was leaning in the direction of a new "triangular" infantry division, with three 75mm gun battalions (12 guns in each battalion) for direct support of the three infantry regiments and a 105mm howitzer battalion for general support. Lacking enough 105mm howitzers, the old Schneider 155mm howitzer was the substitute. However, many artillery officers argued that the 75mm gun lacked the firepower needed on the modern battlefield, and proposed using a 105mm howitzer as the primary field gun in the division, with a battalion of 155mm howitzers for general support. This configuration gained considerable support after the fall of France in June 1940, when it received the backing of the G-3 (Operations and Training Section) of the General Staff.

The infantry branch of the Army fostered the development of a number of weapons separate from the artillery branch; mainly small, lightweight weapons used in the frontlines for direct support. The main focus of infantry interest in the 1920s was the development of a new 75mm pack howitzer that could be broken down into several loads and transported by horse or mule.

The 1930s were a time of great ferment in the artillery branch, even if equipment modernization was slowed by a lack of funding. The groundwork was laid for the most important tactical innovation, the Fire Direction Center (FDC), a critical ingredient in artillery fire support in mobile warfare. Instead of each battery commander having control over the firing decision, new methods were developed to allow an artillery battalion to rapidly mass its fire against a single target and shift it rapidly if needed. The battalion FDC would deploy a forward observer to determine accurately the location of the target; this system was later enhanced, beginning in June 1942, by using forward observers in light aircraft, who could locate targets out of the visual range of ground observers. The fielding of tactical radios also allowed the forward observers to rapidly communicate with the battalion FDC, and to move when necessary without the encumbrance of field telephone wires. The FDC also centralized the computation of firing data to permit its batteries to engage on a single target within ten minutes of the fire call from the forward observer. The battalion FDC was adopted in 1941, and a divisional FDC was first demonstrated the same year. The FDC innovation proved vital in the campaign in Tunisia in 1943 and Gen Bradley noted that it permitted any forward observer to bring the fire of the entire corps artillery, some 324 guns and howitzers, against a single target. Artillery proved itself invaluable again and again in the subsequent campaigns due to excellent training, tactics, and technology.

The start of the war in Europe in September 1939 encouraged the US Army to begin a substantial expansion of its artillery. In 1937, the Army fielded only 25 field artillery battalions, but by the outbreak of war in December 1941 this number had increased fivefold to 142 battalions, and eventually totaled over 700 battalions by 1945.

US DIVISIONAL FIELD ARTILLERY

The 75mm Pack Howitzer

The US Army had begun development of a new pack howitzer prior to World War I to replace the British Vickers-Maxim 2.95-in. gun then in use. Pack howitzers were mainly intended for use in mountainous or other difficult terrain where towed field guns were impractical. The weapons received their name from the ability to disassemble them into several loads that could be carried on packs by horses or mules; most other armies called these weapons mountain guns. Development of the 75mm Pack Howitzer M1 began in 1920 and was completed in 1927. Although the M1 was standardized in August 1927, funding was so limited that large-scale production never took place. Under the 1925 Ten-Year Ordnance Plan, the Army proposed acquiring 48 guns, enough for two regiments. However, by 1933 only 32 had been manufactured or funded. Production of the 75mm pack howitzer totaled only 91 by 1940. Because of the long delay in entering serial production, improvements were gradually introduced into the weapon, primarily concerning the breech ring and breech block. The modified version was designated as the 75mm Pack Howitzer M1A1 and eventually became the primary version of this weapon.

The 75mm Field Howitzer M1A1 could be distinguished from its pack howitzer relatives by the use of the M3A1 carriage with split trails. (Author's collection)

During World War II, the need emerged for a lightweight howitzer to support the new airborne forces. The M1A1 was an obvious solution, but the wooden-spoked wheels of the M1 carriage were a bit archaic. As a result, the M8 (airborne) carriage was adopted in its place, which introduced modern pneumatic tires and new axle bearings but was otherwise the same. It is worth noting here that during this period the Ordnance Department employed the cumbersome practice of designating artillery weapons by gun and carriage. So the airborne version of the pack howitzer was officially designated as 75mm Pack Howitzer M1A1 on Carriage (airborne) M8. The usual convention is to shorten this to the weapon designation alone, which will be the practice followed here, except when the need arises to specify the carriage type.

After very limited production in the interwar years, large-scale manufacture of the M1A1 pack howitzer did not resume until September 1940. Total production of the M1A1, primarily on the M8 carriage, totaled 4,939 weapons by the time manufacture ended in December 1944, making it the second most common US howitzer of the war. Although manufactured in very large numbers, the 75mm pack howitzer did not see correspondingly widespread deployment, equipping only 36 battalions in 1944–45. It was used primarily by the artillery battalions of the airborne and mountain divisions, with some 22 divisional battalions in Europe and three in the Pacific. Its compact size made it suitable for use in mountainous and jungle terrain, so it also equipped two non-divisional field artillery battalions in Italy and four in the Pacific.

The US Marine Corps decided to replace its French 75mm M1897 guns with the 75mm pack howitzer in the summer of 1930. When the Marines adopted a divisional organization in February 1941, there was an artillery regiment in each of the new divisions with three 75mm pack howitzer battalions. These were gradually upgraded with the more powerful 105mm howitzer, so by the time of the Saipan campaign in the summer of 1944, the artillery regiments had two 75mm pack howitzer and two 105mm howitzer battalions each. By the time of the Iwo Jima battle in 1945, only one 75mm pack howitzer battalion remained in the Marine artillery regiments, though the 75mm "Tiny Tims" of the 1/11th Marines were extremely popular, since their small size and ample supplies of ammunition made them a very handy weapon for direct-fire support in the bitter fighting.

The US Army began to modernize its large inventory of M1897 75mm guns for motorized traction in the mid-1930s. This is the basic M1897A4, which retained the original box-trail carriage but substituted pneumatic tires for the wooden wheels of the original gun. This battery is seen during a summer exercise at Pine Camp in upstate New York in 1935. (NARA)

Cavalry Cannon: the 75mm Field Howitzer M1A1

During the 1920s, the cavalry branch of the Army noted the configuration of the infantry's 75mm pack howitzer and realized it would make an ideal light howitzer if modified to permit high-speed towing. Since weight was not as constrained as for a mountain gun, the cavalry preferred a more conventional split trail to provide better stability when firing. The new carriage was designated as the Carriage M3A1 and featured spindles to permit the pneumatic wheels to be raised, and a firing base lowered to provide a three-point suspension when firing. In spite of cavalry interest in this weapon, no significant production of the 75mm Field Howitzer M1A1 took place until after the start of World War II. Serial manufacture began in January 1941, but lasted only a year, during which time only 298 were manufactured. Modest improvements were made to the carriage, notably the addition of a gun shield, resulting in the M3A2 carriage, and the substitution of combat tires and divided rims, becoming the M3A3 carriage. Although standardized, only 51 of these were manufactured in April–May 1943 before production was again ended, making them among the rarest US howitzers of World War II. Nearly a third of the howitzers were provided to China during the war.

The M1A1 field howitzer does not appear to have been widely used by the US Army during the war, but records seldom distinguish between this weapon and the related pack howitzer. The premature close of production of this field howitzer was due to the growing mechanization of the cavalry and the preference for a self-propelled weapon. The first expedient version of this was the T30 75mm Howitzer Motor Carriage (HMC), which combined the M1A1 field gun on an M3 half-track. These were used in mechanized cavalry units as well as in some light tank battalions as an assault gun and in infantry cannon companies. It was followed by the M8 75mm HMC, which mounted the 75mm gun in an open turret on the M5 light tank chassis. This particular vehicle was most commonly used in mechanized cavalry reconnaissance squadrons as an assault gun to provide additional firepower to the unit's M8 light armored cars.

The French Mademoiselle: the 75mm Gun

The most common artillery weapon in service in the US Army through the interwar years was the 75mm Gun M1897, popularly dubbed the "French Mademoiselle" by the gunners of the AEF. Although the Westervelt Board leaned towards the adoption of the heavier 105mm caliber for the standard divisional artillery piece, the US Army in the 1920s had an ample supply of French- and American-built 75mm M1897s on hand. From 1920 to 1925, the Ordnance Department modernized this weapon with a new split-trail carriage, the M1923E, that was standardized in 1926 as the 75mm Gun M1 on Carriage M2A1. Although a battery of these was completed in 1926, conversion was slowed by the lack of funding. With the advent of new projectiles with improved high-explosive fills such as TNT, a modified gun

The most extensive modernization of the French *"soixante-quinze"* was the 75mm Gun M1897A2 on the new split trail M2A3 carriage. Many of these upgrades were undertaken in 1941 as an effort to field an expedient antitank gun. (NARA)

was developed in 1932 and accepted for small-scale production in 1936 as the 75mm Gun M2. Although the artillery had been slow to embrace motorization in the 1920s, in 1933 the new Chief of Staff, Gen Douglas MacArthur, ordered the motorization of half of its light field artillery. This program took two forms: the conversion of the original box-trail carriage into the M1897A4 with a "high-speed" adapter, including new bearings and pneumatic tires, and conversion of other pieces using newly manufactured M2A1 carriages with split trails. Starting in 1936, the Army motorized 56 of its 81 75mm gun battalions with these two versions of the venerable French 75mm gun.

Shortly after the fall of France in June 1940, the US Army realized it was perilously short of modern antitank guns, and so a crash program was started to convert the M1897 75mm gun into an antitank weapon. Two carriages were used: the slightly improved M2A2, and the M2A3 carriage that had a drawbar for use in motorized towing; both had direct-fire sights. From July 1940 to November 1941 a total of 918 of the 2,800 75mm M1897 guns on hand were converted. Although nominally intended as an antitank gun, the rebuilt weapons were issued to field artillery units as well in the early months of the war due to the desperate shortage of modern equipment.

Although the 75mm gun was scheduled to be replaced by the 105mm howitzer in divisional artillery battalions, the delay in the start of production meant that the 75mm gun in its various forms remained in service at the time of the Pearl Harbor attack in December 1941. As a result, the 75mm gun saw combat in small numbers during the Philippines fighting in December 1941 as well as with the 2/131st Field Artillery in the Dutch East Indies.

US FIELD ARTILLERY PRODUCTION IN WORLD WAR II

	1940	1941	1942	1943	1944	1945	Total
75mm Pack Howitzer M1A1	36	188	1,208	2,592	915	0	4,939
75mm Field Howitzer M1A1	0	234	64	51	0	0	349
105mm Howitzer M2A1	0	597	3,325	2,684	1,200	730	8,536
105mm Howitzer M3	0	0	0	1,965	410	205	2,580
4.5-in. Field Gun M1	0	0	41	345	40	0	426
155mm Howitzer M1	0	0	19	1,469	1,949	598	4,035
155mm Gun M1A1	3	62	439	598	526	254	1,882
8-in. Howitzer M1	0	0	132	142	554	178	1,006
8-in. Gun M1	0	0	10	49	57	23	139
240mm Howitzer M1	0	0	6	57	158	94	315
Total	**39**	**1,081**	**5,244**	**9,952**	**5,809**	**2,082**	**24,207**

Army Workhorse: the 105mm Howitzer M2A1

The 105mm Howitzer M2 was without question the single most important US Army field artillery piece of World War II, and so its origins are worth some detailed examination. The Westervelt Board noted that the German, Austrian, and Italian armies had used a 105mm light field howitzer during World War I and that the British had used a similar 4.5-in. howitzer as well. The board recommended a 105mm howitzer as the ideal divisional weapon but, recognizing the financial burden of switching from 75mm to 105mm, suggested at least that it would be a better substitute for the Schneider 155mm howitzer in one of the division's artillery battalions. The

The original 105mm Howitzer M1920 bears little resemblance to its eventual World War II descendent. This pilot weapon is seen with the T2 Cutts Compensator, an early type of muzzle brake to reduce the recoil force. (USAOM-APG)

board also recommended that a new carriage developed for the 105mm howitzer could be used to mount a modernized 75mm divisional gun.

After studying captured German 105mm howitzers, the Ordnance Department developed the 105mm Howitzer Model 1920 on Carriage Model 1920. The design employed split trails rather than the box-trail design favored by the French. An evaluation by the Field Artillery Board in April 1923 found the design to be too heavy and clumsy, and unsuitable for adoption, but it was impressed by the split-trail design. A box-trail carriage was also developed, the Model 1921E, but the board turned down this design as well, preferring the new split-trail configuration. In spite of the board's recommendation, the Ordnance Department submitted another box-trail design, the Model 1925E carriage. Two other rival designs were also developed at this time, the T1 and T2 carriages, which were split-trail types. The new split-trail carriages had been designed with the board's earlier recommendations in mind, and in particular, the need for a recoil system that would not require a large pit to be dug under the weapon when the gun was elevated to the maximum. Although it still had problems, the T2 and the associated 105mm howitzer were standardized in December 1927 as the Carriage, Recoil Mechanism and Howitzer, all Model M1. However, as production funding was unavailable and development work was still underway, no M1 howitzers were ever manufactured. In 1929, this situation forced the Army to revert to its World War I-era reliance on 75mm guns and 155mm howitzers in a mix of two 75mm gun regiments and one 155mm gun regiment in each divisional artillery brigade.

During the early 1930s, the Ordnance Department developed the T1 cartridge case, a semi-fixed type shell that allowed the crew to load the ammunition in one piece rather than the previous split case in which the shell and propellant charge were loaded separately. Since the chamber of the howitzer tube needed to be changed, the modified howitzer was redesignated as the 105mm Howitzer M2. A number of muzzle brakes were also developed and tested in the hope

The 105mm howitzer begins to evolve into its eventual configuration, as seen here during the 1932 trials of the 105mm Howitzer M2 on Carriage M1. Fourteen of these were manufactured in the early 1930s, the only serial production of the type until the outbreak of World War II. (USAOM-APG)

of reducing the recoil force of the weapon, but this project was canceled in April 1933. The 1925 Ten-Year Ordnance Plan envisioned manufacturing 72 105mm howitzers to equip three regiments, but by 1933 only 14 M1 carriages had been manufactured.

Trials of the 105mm Howitzer M2 on Carriage M1 were conducted in 1932 at Fort Sill using a six-horse team. The testing revealed that the M2 howitzer was generally satisfactory except that improvements were needed in the recoil system, with the M1E5 type preferred. The M1 carriage was the main source of problems, being unsuitable for motorized towing and having other flaws. As a result, two alternative carriages were developed and delivered to Aberdeen Proving Ground in February 1938 for trials as the T3 and T4. With the US Army now favoring motorized towing for divisional artillery, the new T4 carriage featured reduced weight and was the preferred type. An improved design, the T5, was submitted alongside a modified T4E1 carriage in the next round of tests in November 1939.

In spite of the imperfect design, the Army wanted production to begin as soon as possible and ordered the first production batch of 48 M2 howitzers in 1939. The tests favored the new T5 carriage, which was standardized on February 23, 1940, as the M2. Prior to the start of large-scale production, some minor changes were made to the howitzer breech ring, resulting in the M2A1 in March 1940, which became the standard version of this weapon. This led to the basic configuration of the classic 105mm howitzer, the 105mm Howitzer M2A1 on Carriage M2. Serial production of this design began in April 1941.

By the time that the 105mm howitzer was ready for production, the Army had come to accept it as the future basis for divisional artillery, replacing the 75mm gun in three battalions in each division for direct support, with a 155mm howitzer battalion providing general support. The 105mm caliber was also standard in the Wehrmacht, but the other Allied armies preferred smaller divisional weapons, the British favoring the 25-pdr and the Red Army favoring the 76mm divisional gun. By the time that the 105mm M2A1 howitzer had entered production, the US Army had decided that all divisional artillery should be motorized. The standard prime mover for the 105mm howitzer was the short-wheelbase 2½-ton truck.

Development of the 105mm howitzer continued even after production began. On reports of the success of the British 25-pdr with its box-trail design, a similar design with a firing platform was built as the M2E1 carriage. This configuration received little support and was canceled in September 1943. Another source of foreign inspiration was the M2E2 carriage, which used folding spades like the German lFH 18 105mm howitzer. The use of a muzzle brake was revised, producing the 105mm Howitzer M2A1E1, but it was never accepted for production. The only major changes incorporated into the design during the war affected the carriage. In November

The first series production version of the 105mm howitzer in World War II was this configuration, the 105mm Howitzer M2A1 on Carriage M2. (USAOM-APG)

The 105mm Howitzer M2A1 on Carriage M2 saw combat use in the early campaigns of World War II, here in Tunisia during the fighting on February 12, 1943. This system still retains the original pattern of commercial tires and the carriage is fitted with brakes for use during motorized towing. (NARA)

1942, the War Department adopted a new policy stating that towed vehicles under 5,000lb (2,273kg) were not required to be equipped with power-operated brakes activated from the prime mover. As a result, the brakes on the M2 carriage were deleted, resulting in the M2A1 carriage in May 1943. In August 1942, Gen Lesley McNair of Army Ground Forces requested that the artillery branch study better shields on field artillery weapons. An improved shield along with an enclosed screw traverse mechanism was incorporated into the new M2A2 carriage, which was standardized in August 1943. There was a program to upgrade all the M2 and M2A1 carriages to the M2A2 standards, though this was not completed in view of the number of artillery pieces already deployed overseas.

In total, some 8,536 M2A1 105mm howitzers were manufactured from April 1941 to June 1945, making it the most widely produced US field artillery piece of World War II. It was also the most widely used US field artillery piece of the war, equipping 264 field artillery battalions, including 147 divisional battalions and 14 non-divisional battalions in the ETO and 62 divisional and nine non-divisional battalions in the Pacific. The Marine Corps began deploying the 105mm howitzer in

In May 1943, the M2 carriage was modified by deleting the Warner electric brakes previously fitted. Some M2 carriages like this one were modified to M2A1 standards after construction, as is evident here from the remaining battery box on the right trail, which was deleted on new construction M2A1 carriages. Also worth noting is the use of combat tires, a widespread improvement on US field artillery by 1943. This howitzer is from the 522d Field Artillery Battalion attached to the Japanese-American 442d Infantry (Nisei-Separate) near Bruyeres, France, on October 18, 1944. (NARA)

The 105mm Howitzer M2A1 on Carriage M2A2 adopted an auxiliary splinter shield in front of the main shield to protect the crew better when the weapon was traversed. This example is seen with the gun tube in full recoil while conducting a fire mission near La Neuveville, France, on October 6, 1944. (NARA)

1942, and each division began with one 105mm howitzer battalion of the four battalions in its artillery regiment. By the time of the 1944 campaigns on Saipan and Guam, this ratio had been raised to two of four, and by Iwo Jima in 1945, to three of four, eventually completely replacing the smaller 75mm pack howitzer.

Infantry Cannon: the 105mm Howitzer M3

With the organization of new airborne regiments underway in 1941, there was a requirement for a 105mm howitzer that could be delivered by aircraft. The existing M2 105mm howitzer was clearly too large, so in August 1941 initial designs were made using the 105mm howitzer shortened by 27in. (68.6cm), mounted on the sleigh of the M1A2 recoil mechanism from the 75mm howitzer. The modified weapon was fitted to the M3A1 carriage of the 75mm field howitzer. A pilot version of the 105mm Howitzer T7 was sent to Aberdeen Proving Ground in March 1942. The main failing of the design was that the slow powder used in the standard M2A1 howitzer shells gave unsatisfactory results in the shortened version, producing excessive muzzle blast and flash, and incomplete burning of the propellant. This was a significant issue, since it had been the hope that the new weapon could use the 105mm ammunition already in service. Nevertheless, the design itself proved very satisfactory and the performance was acceptable if using fast-burning propellant. As a result, the weapon was standardized as the 105mm Howitzer M3 on carriages M3 and M3A1. The M3 carriage was basically the existing M3A1 carriage of the 75mm field howitzer, which used $\frac{3}{32}$-in. (2mm) plate for the trails, and this configuration was designated as substitute standard. The preferred standard configuration was the new M3A1 carriage, which used $\frac{1}{8}$-in. (3mm) plate for the trails. Production began in February 1943, ended in May 1944, and was resumed in April–June 1945, with total production amounting to 2,580 howitzers.

In service, the main fault of the weapon was the weakness of the trails, which is not surprising since they had originally been developed for a much less powerful 75mm howitzer. A tubular trail configuration was designed, but did not enter production. Other improvements considered for the weapon included an increase in elevation up to 65 degrees (studied on the 105mm Howitzer T10), the addition of shields to protect the crew on the M3A2 carriage, and improvements in the recoil mechanism. In service use, the standard prime mover for this howitzer was the $1\frac{1}{2}$-ton truck.

Although originally designed for airborne use, the weapon was also authorized for the cannon companies of infantry regiments. A cannon company was authorized under the new triangular infantry division table of organization of April 1, 1942, even though the weapon was not yet available. As a result, divisions with cannon companies, such as those deployed to Tunisia in 1942–43, were generally equipped with substitutes. For example, the cannon companies of the 1st Infantry Division had two platoons of T30 75mm HMC (three per platoon) and one platoon of T19 105mm HMC (two per platoon). These HMCs were the 75mm pack howitzer and 105mm howitzer on an expedient M3 half-track mount. The self-propelled cannon companies were again used on Sicily in July 1943. However, artillery commanders were unhappy about this substitute equipment, as it encouraged the infantry to sidetrack them for other missions, including use as tank hunters. In March 1943, the Army Ground Forces headquarters tried to have the cannon companies eliminated, but they remained under the revised infantry tables of organization from September 1943. With the towed M3 105mm howitzer finally available, these cannon companies were reorganized, each having six howitzers in three platoons, with two howitzers in each platoon. There were some alterations to this organization in the field: for example, the use of M7 105mm HMCs in some infantry divisions in the Philippines in 1944–45.

The 105mm Howitzer M3 was the standard weapon in infantry cannon companies by the time of the D-Day landings in France. This one, nicknamed "Hitler's Doom" is seen in action with the 9th Cannon Company, 2d Infantry Division, near Brest on August 28, 1944. (NARA)

Even though developed on the basis of an airborne requirement, the M3 105mm howitzer was slow in entering paratroop service, as the 75mm pack howitzer was easier to transport. At the time of the Normandy airborne landings, the pattern was to mimic the normal infantry division scheme but with lighter weapons: three field artillery battalions with the 75mm pack howitzer for direct support, and one of the glider artillery battalions with the M3 105mm howitzer for general divisional support. This was an expedient organization and was not officially authorized for the airborne division's glider field artillery battalion until the modification of the table of organization on December 16, 1944. Unlike the infantry cannon companies, the airborne units used the jeep as the prime mover for the 105mm howitzer.

Legacy Weapons: the Schneider 155mm Howitzer

The AEF received 747 French Schneider 155mm M1917 howitzers for use during the 1918 campaigns of World War I, and licensed production had begun in the United States in 1917 on a slightly modified version, the M1918, with a modified breech assembly and simpler shield design.

There were a number of attempts to develop lightweight recoilless artillery weapons during World War II, like this 105mm Howitzer T9, seen here folded up in traveling mode. None of the recoilless field-artillery types reached combat service during the war, but they pioneered the way for postwar weapons. (USAOM-APG)

	75mm pack howitzer	105mm howitzer	105mm howitzer	155mm howitzer
Cannon type	M1A1	M2A1	M3	M1
Carriage type	M8 airborne	M2A2	M3	M1
Weight (lb/kg)	1,440/653	4,980/2,260	955/433	11,966/5,427
Length (ft/m)	12.1/3.7	19.6/6.0	12.9/3.9	24/7.3
Width (ft/m)	4/1.2	7.04/2.14	5.6/1.7	7.95/2.4
Length of bore (calibers)	15.9	22.5	16.5	20
Max. elevation (degrees)	45	66	65	65
Max. powder pressure (lb/sq. in.)	26,000	30,000	25,000	32,000
Breech type	Sliding wedge	Sliding wedge	Sliding wedge	Interrupted thread
Rate of fire	8rds/30sec	2–4rpm	15rpm	2rpm
Max. range (yds/km)	9,760/8.9	12,205/11.1	8,295/7.85	16,000/14.6
Recoil type	Hydropneumatic	Hydropneumatic	Hydropneumatic	Hydropneumatic
Type of ammunition	Semi-fixed	Semi-fixed	Semi-fixed	Separate
HE projectile type	M48	M1	M1	M107
Projectile weight (lb/kg)	14.6/6.6	33/14.9	33/14.9	95/43.1
HE fill (lb/kg)	1.5/0.66	4.8/2.2	4.8/2.2	15.8/7.2
Propellant weight (lb/kg)	0.92/0.41	3.66/1.66	1.32/.06	13.4/6.1

A regiment was equipped with the American-manufactured howitzers in August 1918, but it did not arrive in France until after the Armistice. Under the recommendations of the Westervelt Board, the plan in the early 1920s was to shift this weapon from divisional level to corps level (due to its size and power) once the 105mm howitzer became available. When the 105mm program was delayed due to lack of funds, in 1929 the 155mm howitzer reverted back to divisional use. Owing to the financial constraints, there was no serious effort to develop a new 155mm howitzer during the interwar years. However, MacArthur's 1933 decision to motorize the field artillery included plans to modernize 75 percent of the divisional weapons as soon as funds became available. Development of a new carriage began in 1934, and it introduced pneumatic tires, anti-friction bearings, and air brakes for motorized towing. The M1918A1 carriage was standardized in 1936 and by 1940, 599 howitzers of the

A 155mm howitzer with the "high-speeded" M1918A1 carriage in action with the 6th Field Artillery Battalion, 1st Infantry Division, at El Guettar on March 23, 1943. The defeat of the 10th Panzer Division at El Guettar that day was the first US victory in Tunisia and was widely attributed to the superb performance of the field artillery. (NARA)

2,971 in service had been "high-speeded." Further improvements were introduced on the M1918A3 carriage, which included torque rods.

Since production of a new 155mm howitzer was not likely until late 1942, the Army felt it would be prudent to modernize much of the remainder of the inventory. This program started in 1940 with 35 more howitzers modernized, followed by 1,162 in 1941 and 218 by May 1942, adding a further 1,415 "high-speeded" 155mm howitzers to the inventory for a grand total of 2,014. These saw widespread combat duty in the first years of the war, including use in the Philippines and the Dutch East Indies in 1941–42, in the Pacific campaigns in 1942–43, and in Tunisia in 1942–43. As the new M1 155mm howitzer became available after October 1942, the old Schneider field howitzer was replaced. However, some theaters with lower priority kept the weapon in service. So, for example, there were still some Schneiders in use with the Fifth Army in Italy in the winter of 1943–44 and this weapon was widely used in the Pacific in the 1943 fighting.

The 155mm Howitzer M1

A shortage of funds meant there were few development efforts to replace the Schneider 155mm howitzer in the interwar years. The Westervelt Board's recommendations led to the idea of developing a common new carriage that could be used with either the 4.7-in. gun or 155mm howitzer, but the howitzer requirement received low priority. This was caused in part by the bitter debate about whether the 155mm howitzer should remain in the infantry division or be relegated to corps support. One of the widely acknowledged problems with the Schneider was its limited traverse, which necessitated moving the entire weapon for changes of more than three degrees. In 1934, the modern T2 split-trail carriage was developed to solve this problem, but in 1939 the program came under question, since it seemed rather pointless to fit such an antiquated cannon to such a modern carriage. As a result, the project was restarted with the intention of fielding not only a new carriage, but also a new howitzer.

Since by this time the 155mm howitzer had an established place as a divisional weapon, an important aspect of the program was to reduce the weight of the weapon using more modern recuperators and trunnion

assemblies. Work on the weapon proceeded very smoothly and the new 155mm Howitzer M1 on Carriage M1 was standardized on May 15, 1941. However, manufacture of the M1 howitzer was badly delayed by the production bottlenecks caused by the rapid expansion of US war outputs in 1941 to meet the imminent threat of conflict. Manufacture of the 155mm howitzer did not begin until October 1942, as the Army placed priority on the new 155mm howitzer and 155mm gun. Production finally began to catch up by the middle of 1943, so that by D-Day the US infantry divisions deploying to France had been reequipped with this new weapon. Coincidentally, the delay in production of the howitzer matched delays in fielding a suitable prime mover, the M5 HST. Although the howitzer could be towed by trucks, the preferred solution was the M5 HST, and most battalions equipped with the new howitzer also received the new prime mover. Manufacture of the 155mm Howitzer M1 continued through June 1945, by which time some 4,035 were fielded, making it the third most commonly produced American field artillery piece of the war after the 105mm howitzer and 75mm pack howitzer.

The M1 155mm howitzer was the second most commonly used US field artillery piece of the war, with some 170 field artillery battalions formed. Among these, 49 divisional and 78 non-divisional battalions served in the European campaigns, and 22 divisional and 14 non-divisional in the Pacific. US infantry divisions usually deployed three 105mm and one 155mm howitzer battalions. As was noted, there were actually more non-divisional 155mm howitzer battalions in service in Europe, and these units were the mainstay of corps artillery support. The Marine Corps was slower to adopt the 155mm howitzer, due to its tighter logistics restrictions,

A camouflaged battery of 155mm M1 howitzers of the 20th Field Artillery Battalion, 4th Infantry Division, in action near St. Lo on July 24, 1944, during Operation *Cobra*, the break-out from Normandy. (NARA)

but by the summer of 1944 it had begun to deploy several 155mm howitzer battalions under their corps artillery. During the Saipan campaign one of these corps' 155mm howitzer battalions was administratively attached to reinforce the divisional artillery.

US CORPS HEAVY ARTILLERY

The Forgotten Caliber: the 4.5-in. Gun and Rockets

During World War I, the AEF had employed the 4.7-in. Model 1906 gun, and the Westervelt Board recommended that a modernized version be developed. The Ordnance Department designed the 4.7-in. Gun M1920 on Carriage M1920, which evolved into the 4.7-in. Gun M1922E on Carriage M1921E. This carriage could also be adapted to a new 155mm howitzer. Although the Field Artillery Board recommended that the M1922E be standardized, a lack of funding continued to pose a major problem. The Ten-Year Ordnance Plan recommended that 24 be manufactured to equip a regiment, but this never took place.

The 4.7-in. gun requirement was revived in 1939 alongside the program to develop a new 155mm howitzer for the T2 split-trail carriage. The 4.7-in. Gun T3 was a resurrection of the M1922E, and Ordnance recommended its standardization in January 1940. However, with danger looming in Europe, the artillery branch raised the issue of whether it might be better to change the caliber to 4.5in. to ensure commonality with the British. This was accepted and the modified weapon was standardized in April 1941 as the 4.5-in. Field Gun M1. In spite of its early acceptance, the 4.5-in. gun received very little priority, as production of the much more powerful 155mm Gun M1A1 was already

The 4.5-in. field gun was nearly identical to the more common 155mm howitzer except for its longer gun tube. This is the T1 pilot gun seen on trials at Aberdeen Proving Ground in November 1941. (USAOM-APG)

The 4.5-in. T32 Xylophone artillery rocket launcher was the only US Army rocket artillery deployed in significant numbers by the Army's field artillery battalions during the war. Some are seen here in action with Battery A, 18th Field Artillery Battalion, near Kleinhau on November 26, 1944. (NARA)

underway for corps support requirements. The 4.5-in. caliber straddled the two main US Army calibers: 105mm and 155mm, and the Army Ground Forces favored standardization. Indeed, it is not clear at all why any production took place. In the event, the 4.5-in. field gun entered production alongside its twin, the 155mm howitzer, in September 1942. However, only 426 were completed by February 1944, when production ended. In spite of the small number manufactured, 16 field artillery battalions were equipped with the 4.5-in. field gun, all being deployed to the European Theater of Operations (ETO) in June–October 1944 for corps support. As in the case of the 155mm howitzer, the standard prime mover was the M5 HST. This weapon was hastily retired in 1945 as field commanders argued that it was no better than the more common 155mm howitzer, simply complicating ammunition supply.

Other 4.5-in. artillery weapons manufactured in World War II were a variety of 4.5-in. rocket launchers. Although the history of US Army rocket development in World War II is too complicated to relate here in detail, it is worth noting that the 4.5-in. rocket launchers were the only types deployed by US Army field artillery. The 4.5-in. rocket was first deployed on a trial basis with the 12th Field Artillery Battalion during the siege of Brest in the summer of 1944, but its experimental T27 frame launcher proved unsuitable. The principal field artillery type was the 4.5-in. T32 Xylophone launcher, which consisted of four sets of eight 7½ft (2.3m) launch tubes for a total of 32 tubes, mounted laterally on the rear of a 2½-ton truck, and firing the fin-stabilized M8 4.5-in. rocket. A total of 75 launchers were issued to the 18th Field Artillery Battalion, which deployed them in combat in November 1944 near the Siegfried Line, and again during the Ardennes campaign. The improved T66 Honeycomb launcher with 24 tubes on a two-wheeled carriage, firing the spin-stabilized M16 4.5-in. rockets, was deployed experimentally in the final weeks of the war in Europe and used on at least one occasion in Czechoslovakia in May 1945. Five more rocket battalions were organized in 1945, each equipped with the Honeycomb launcher; two battalions were forward deployed to the Philippines and Okinawa but not in time to take part in combat. The US Marine Corps also organized their own rocket detachments in 1945, using Navy-developed launchers on ¾- and 2½-ton trucks.

The Xylophone was followed by the T66 Honeycomb towed rocket launcher, which fired the M16 spin-stabilized 4.5-in. rocket. A handful saw service in May 1945 in Czechoslovakia. (Author's collection)

Legacy Gun: the 155mm GPF

During World War I, the AEF used the French 155mm GPF gun as its standard corps gun, and 48 M1917s were acquired directly from France. As in the case of so many other weapons, licensed manufacture was initiated in 1917, but no guns were delivered to the AEF prior to the November 1918 Armistice. As of June 1940, some 973 were still in service, primarily the US-built M1918M1 gun, making it the most common US heavy artillery type at the outbreak of the war. Motorized towing of this large weapon had very low priority and a high-speed carriage was not developed until 1937. Two versions were fielded which both had the same upgrades, including pneumatic tires and air brakes, but the M2 carriage was based on the French M1917 carriage, while the M3 was based on the more common US M1918 or M1918A1 carriages. Modernization of these weapons did not begin on a large scale until 1941, and in total, 598 were converted through July 1942.

As its replacement, the 155mm M1 gun, did not enter service in large numbers until 1942, the GPF saw combat in the early campaigns of World War II, including the Philippines in 1941–42 with the 301st Field Artillery Regiment, and with the Army's F/244th Coastal Artillery Battalion and Marine 5th Defense Battalion on Guadalcanal in 1942. Although it was quickly replaced by the 155mm Gun M1A1 in field artillery units being deployed overseas, the GPF was still widely used in the US Army and Marine Corps in the coastal artillery role through the war.

Long Tom: the 155mm Gun M1A1

Work on a replacement for the GPF began in 1920 with the 155mm Gun M1920, but went into limbo, like so many other projects, due to a lack of funding. The program was revived in 1929 as the 155mm Gun T4 on Carriage T2, aimed at extending the effective range of the weapon from 20,000 to 25,000 yards (18.3 to 22.9km). As was the case with the 155mm howitzer and 4.5-in. gun, the new weapon had its own twin, the 8-in. howitzer, which shared a common carriage but differed in the gun tube. The 155mm Gun M1 was standardized in 1938, but serial production had to wait until after the outbreak of war in Europe. No sooner had production started in October 1940 than the Ordnance Department developed a modestly improved gun, the M1A1, that eliminated the

Although the 155mm Gun GPF was not widely deployed by the US Army in combat during World War II, these weapons were sometimes used when captured. This is a 155mm GPFT, the most modern type in French service in 1940, with a new four-wheel configuration for motorized towing. It was captured from Vichy French forces and used in combat in Tunisia by a US field artillery battalion, seen here near Ferryville, Tunisia, in 1943. (NARA)

breech-ring bushing, cutting the breech threads directly into the breech ring. This was standardized on June 12, 1941, by which time only 20 M1s had been manufactured; so the M1A1 became the standard production variation. The gun underwent surprisingly few changes during the war, although various improvements were considered, such as the M1A1E1 with chromium plating applied to the bore, and the M1A1E3 with liquid-injection cooling, both modifications aimed at reducing wear. The only improvement accepted was the M2, which had a simplified method of attaching the breech ring that was standardized on March 15, 1945.

There were a number of modifications and derivatives of the carriage during the war. M1A1s were simply the pilot T2 carriages refurbished for use, and were few in number. A variety of carriages were developed to permit the M1 to be used as a coastal defense weapon but none were standardized. The new M5 heavy carriage limber was developed to speed the emplacement of the gun compared to the basic M2 limber and was standardized in March 1944.

The 155mm GPF remained in use in some secondary roles and is seen here with a US Army coastal artillery battery at Ft. McAndrew near Argentia, Newfoundland, in September 1943. (NARA)

The 155mm M1 gun was so heavy that some special prime mover was considered necessary. Until a suitable prime mover could be deployed, the first battalions used tractors. A variety of commercial heavy trucks were tested, and eventually the US Army settled on the Mack NO 6x6 7½-ton truck as its prime mover until the dedicated M4 HST became available in 1943.

The M1A1 155mm gun was used primarily for corps support and some 49 battalions were raised during the war. Among these, 40 served in Europe and seven in the Pacific. The M1A1 was first deployed to Tunisia in 1943 with the 34th Field Artillery Battalion. It was immediately successful due to its long-range accuracy. If anything, it was too successful, and during the Italian campaign in 1943–44, it was fired at maximum range with supercharge propellant 90 percent of the time instead of the expected 20 percent. As a result, barrel replacement became a major issue. It was one of the most highly regarded artillery pieces of the war, and was widely used afterwards under its postwar designation of 155mm Gun M59.

Heavy Twin: the 8-in. Howitzer M1

The Midvale Steel and Ordnance Co. in Nicetown, Pennsylvania, manufactured the British 8-in. Howitzer Mark VI prior to the US entry into World War II, and so it was one of the few American-manufactured weapons actually to see combat service with the AEF. A total of 96 were shipped to the AEF of the 195 ordered and a further 100 of the Mark VIII½

A dramatic view of a 155mm Gun M1A1 being fired during exercises near Devries in Great Britain in August 1943 with the 190th Field Artillery Battalion. (NARA)

A 155mm Gun M1 is towed ashore from a Landing Craft, Tank (LCT) at Pt. Caronia, Sicily on August 3, 1943. Tractors were used in some units until the standard Mack NO truck and M4 High-Speed Tractor (HST) prime movers became available later in 1943. (NARA)

A fine overview of the 8-in. Howitzer M1 during a demonstration at Aberdeen Proving Ground. The howitzer is seen with the regulation pit under the breech to permit the weapon to be used at maximum elevation. (USAOM-APG)

were ordered but not completed. Including other howitzers provided by Britain directly to the AEF, the US Army had 475 8-in. howitzers on hand in June 1940.

The decision to develop a new 8-in. howitzer was closely tied to the new M1A1 155mm gun mentioned above. These weapons were essentially identical except for the gun tube. After the short-lived M1920 howitzer fell into limbo like the parallel 155mm gun, in 1927 the program was revived resulting first in the T2 howitzer with a centrifugally cast barrel, and then the T3 with a forged and auto-frettaged barrel. Because of a lack of funding, the program had to wait until 1940 for standardization, with the T3 becoming the new 8-in. Howitzer M1. Production of this howitzer had lower priority than the associated 155mm gun, starting almost two years later in July 1942 and totaling 1,006 howitzers when production ended in June 1945. Although the 155mm gun and the 8-in. howitzer were nearly identical, they could not simply swap barrels in the field, as the different weight of the gun tubes and different recoil forces required changes to the recoil system that needed depot work. The first two battalions of 8-in. howitzers were deployed on the Italian front in November 1943, and the guns were very popular due to their accuracy and power.

As in the case of its twin, the 155mm gun, the M1 8-in. howitzer was used primarily for corps support and 59 battalions were raised during the war. Of these, 38 served in Europe and three in the Pacific. The Marine Corps was so impressed by the performance of the 8-in. howitzer on Okinawa that it began efforts to adopt the weapon, though these had not been completed before the end of the war.

TECHNICAL CHARACTERISTICS: US HEAVY ARTILLERY

	155mm gun	8-in. howitzer	8-in. gun	240mm howitzer
Cannon type	M1A1	M1	M1	M1
Carriage type	M1	M1	M2	M1
Recoil mechanism type	M3	M4	M7	M8
Weight (ton/tonne)	20.1/18.2	15.8/14.4	34.6/31.4	29.0/26.3
Length (ft/m)	34.3/10.4	40/12.2	34.1/10.3	27.5/8.4
Width (ft/m)	8.25/2.5	8.25/2.5	9.2/2.8	9.2/2.8
Length of bore (calibers)	45	25	50	–
Max. elevation (degrees)	65	64	50	65
Max. powder pressure (lb/sq. in.)	38,000	33,000	38,000	36,000
Breech type	Interrupted-screw	Interrupted- screw	Interrupted-step thread	Interrupted-step thread
Rate of fire	1rpm	1rd/2min	1rpm	1rd/2min
Max. range (yds/km)	25,395/23.2	18,510/16.9	35,000/32.0	25,225/23.1
Recoil type	Hydropneumatic	Hydropneumatic	Hydropneumatic	Hydropneumatic
Type of ammunition	Separate loading	Separate loading	Separate loading	Separate loading
HE projectile type	M101	M106	M103	M114
Projectile weight (lb/kg)	94.7/42.9	200/90.7	240/108	360/163
HE fill (lb/kg)	15.1/6.8	29.6/13.4	21/9.5	54/24
Propellant weight (lb/kg)	32.2/14.6	107.5/48.8	107/48	78.7/35.6

Black Dragon: the 8-in. Gun and 240mm Howitzer

The AEF received 40 British 9.2-in. heavy howitzers and the Model 1917 was later produced in the United States in small numbers. This type was no longer in service by 1940. The US Army showed greater interest in the French 240mm howitzer, a weapon developed from the experiences of the siege of Port Arthur during the Russo–Japanese War of 1904–05. Licensed production was only starting when the Armistice was signed in 1918, so none were deployed by the AEF. A total of 330 were manufactured in 1918–19, of which 144 were still deemed safe to fire in 1940. The howitzer was a very heavy and cumbersome weapon that was used by special GHQ reserve artillery units. Firing trials of the 240mm M1918 in 1925 revealed numerous problems that could only be overcome by the design of a new weapon. Owing to the weapon's low-priority status and the lack of funds, no further work was accomplished until 1934 when a

An 8-in. Howitzer M1 of the 105th Field Artillery Battalion is towed by an M4 18-ton HST near Carentilly, France on July 31, 1944, during the Normandy campaign. (NARA)

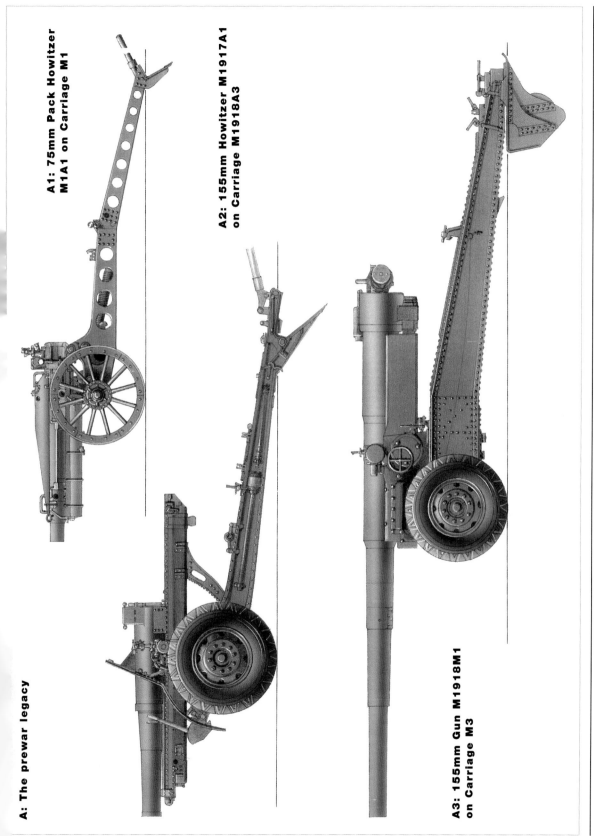

A: The prewar legacy

A1: 75mm Pack Howitzer M1A1 on Carriage M1

A2: 155mm Howitzer M1917A1 on Carriage M1918A3

A3: 155mm Gun M1918M1 on Carriage M3

A

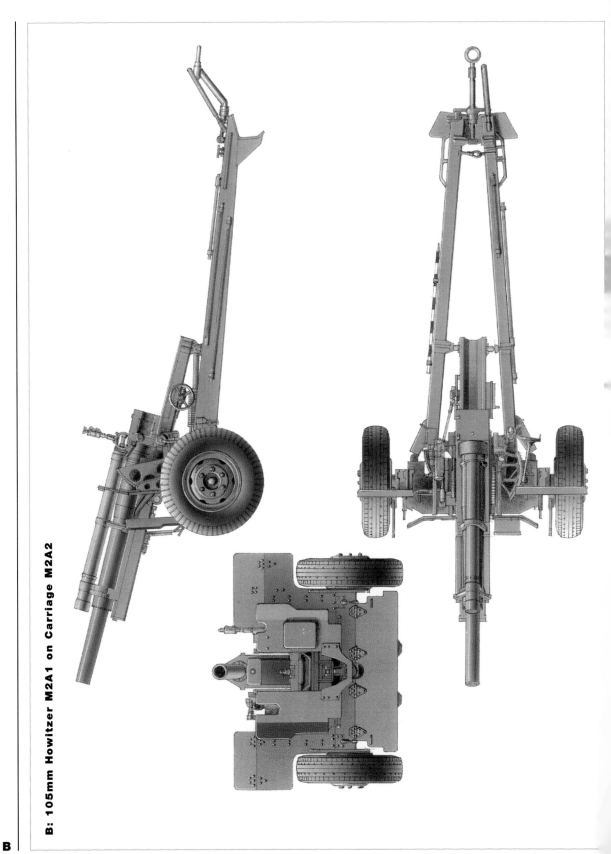

B: 105mm Howitzer M2A1 on Carriage M2A2

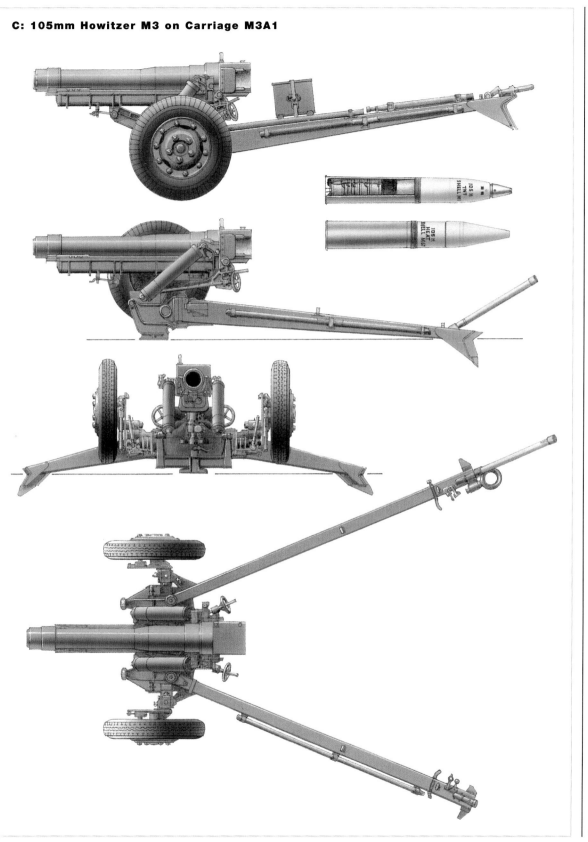

D: 105MM HOWITZER M2A1 ON CARRIAGE M2

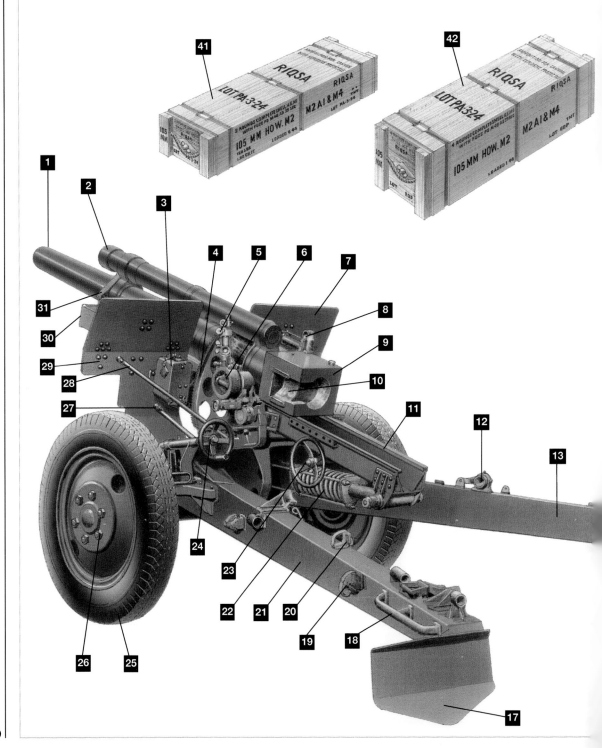

SPECIFICATIONS

Type 105mm Howitzer M2A1 on Carriage M2
Overall weight (lb/kg) 4,980/2,260
Length (ft/m) 19.6/6.0
Width (ft/m) 7.04/2.14
Length of bore (calibers) 22.5
Max. elevation (degrees) 66
Max. powder pressure (lb/sq. in.) 30,000
Breech type Sliding wedge
Rate of fire 2–4rpm
Max. range (yds/km) 12,205/11.1
Recoil type Hydropneumatic
Type of ammunition Semi-fixed
HE projectile type M1
Projectile weight (lb/kg) 33/14.9
HE fill (lb/kg) 4.8/2.2
Propellant weight (lb/kg) 3.66/1.66

KEY

1 Cannon tube
2 Recuperator cylinder
3 Panoramic telescope case
4 Elevating arc
5 M12A2 panoramic telescope
6 M21A1 telescope mount
7 Right upper gun shield flap
8 Breechblock operating handle
9 Breech ring
10 Breech block
11 Cradle
12 Cradle traveling lock
13 Right trail
14 Electrical box for Warner brakes
15 Lunette
16 Drawbar
17 Left spade
18 Crew trail handle
19 Cleaning staff strap
20 Hand spike strap
21 Left trail
22 Equilibrator assembly
23 Left elevating hand-wheel
24 Traversing hand-wheel
25 Tire
26 Wheel disk and rim
27 Lower gun shield brace
28 Upper gun shield brace
29 Upper left shield
30 Cradle
31 Recoil sleigh
32 105mm M67 High-Explosive Anti-Tank (HEAT) Semi-fixed shell
33 105mm M1 High-Explosive shell
34 Cross-section of 105mm propellant cartridge showing propellant bag-charge
35 105mm M84 Smoke Semi-fixed shell
36 M48A2 Point-detonating fuze
37 105mm M1 High-Explosive shell
38 105mm Semi-fixed propellant cartridge
39 Fiberboard transport container for 105mm M1 HE shell
40 M152 105mm ammunition metal container
41 Long 2-round box for 105mm ammunition
42 Long 4-round box for 105mm ammunition

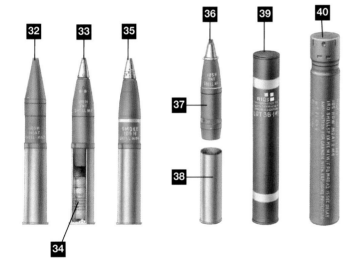

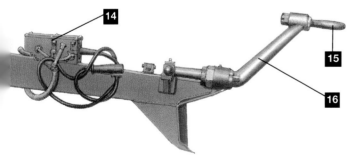

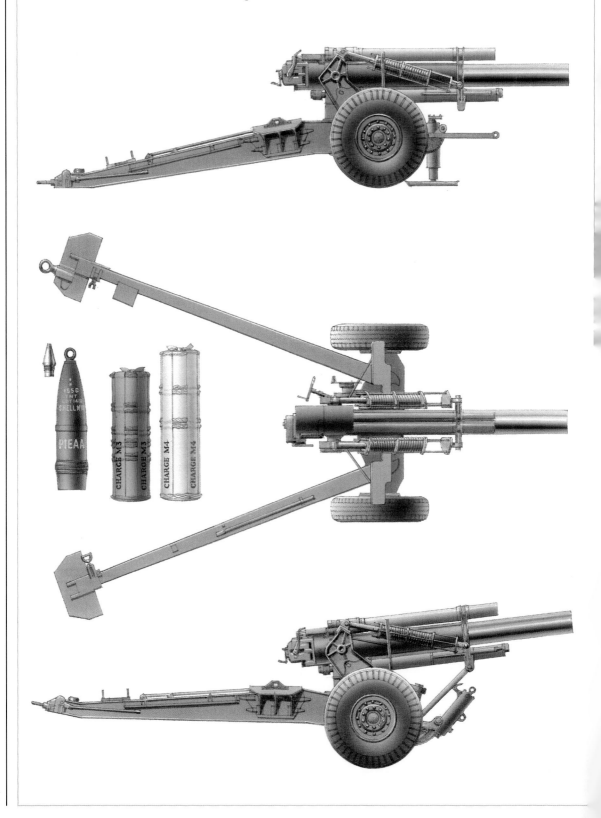

F: 155mm Gun M1A1 on Carriage M1

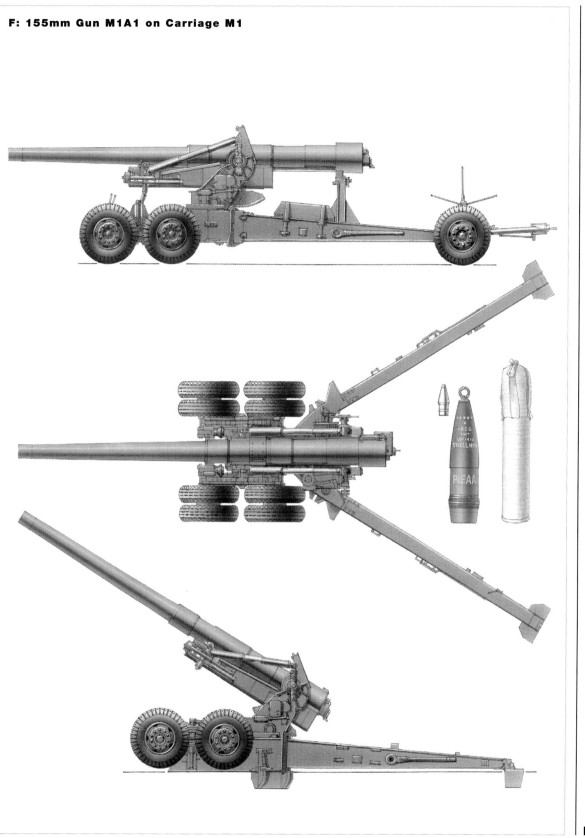

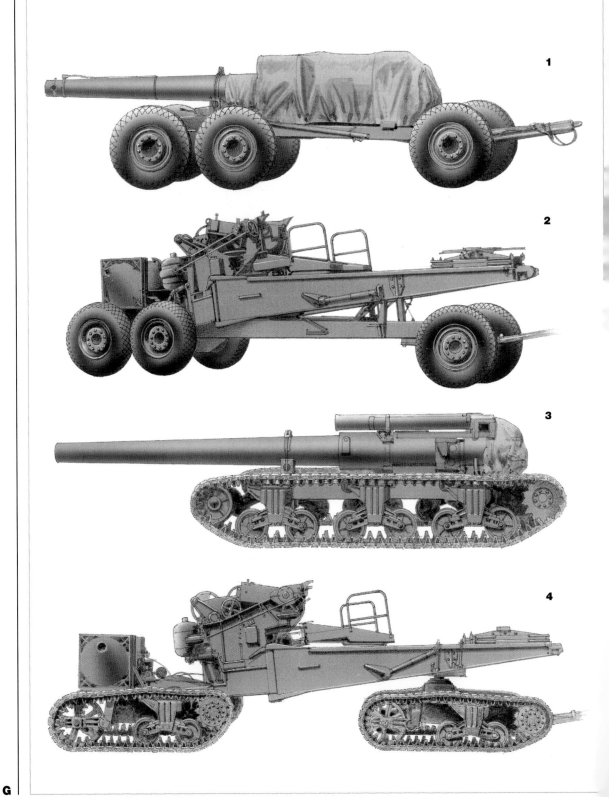

1

2

3

4

Black Dragon, the 240mm howitzer, was the most powerful artillery weapon in US Army service during the war. The size of this massive weapon is evident in this view of a howitzer of the 552d Field Artillery Battalion in France on August 6, 1944. (NARA)

new carriage was designed for motorized towing. This program also went into limbo until funding could be found. Modernized transport wagons were eventually developed for the 240mm Howitzer M1918M1A1, but the 48 sets manufactured were confined to training and coastal defense during World War II and were declared obsolete in 1944.

A new heavy artillery program was started for a third time in April 1940. One of the most challenging aspects of this program was to develop a carriage assembly that would be relatively simple to emplace. To begin with, the 240mm Howitzer T1 would be carried separately on a 4-wheel Howitzer Transport Wagon T2. The carriage was far too heavy and a scheme was designed to use a Heavy Carriage Limber T4 to support the trail ends, and then couple the entire assembly to a T22 tractor. This did not prove entirely satisfactory, so a pair of new three-axle carriage transport wagons were developed that were subsequently standardized as the M2 and the M3.

The entire weapon system was standardized in May 1943 as the 240mm Howitzer M1 on Carriage M1, even though production had already started in November 1942. The delay in production was due mainly to the dismissive attitude of the US Army, which felt that the 155mm gun was as large a weapon as was needed. The Fifth Army in Italy, the first recipient of the 240mm howitzer in the spring of 1944, was reluctant to accept the new battalions. The VI Corps commander, Maj Gen John Lucas, was "doubtful of the value of the 240mm howitzer in this country." Plans to deploy the 240mm howitzer to Italy were delayed by the lack of a suitable prime mover, but the first battalions arrived in Italy in late February 1944. They immediately proved their value due to their ability to demolish key bridges at long range. During the fighting at Cassino, the 240mm howitzers were instrumental in the final reduction of the monastery, already damaged by air attack. In spite of their earlier reluctance, the Fifth Army commanders later dubbed the 240mm howitzer as "the most generally satisfactory weapon" in service in 1944, and it was popularly nicknamed the "Black Dragon" by troops. Ironically, the 240mm howitzer had proven so successful that most of the heavy battalions were allotted to the campaign in France.

A pair of 240mm howitzers from Battery C, 544th Field Artillery Battalion, were used to batter down the northern walls of Manila's walled city on February 22, 1945. This is the later configuration of the 240mm howitzer, with the tracked T17E1 transport wagon evident to the left. (NARA)

The 240mm howitzer was the most unwieldy weapon deployed by the US field artillery in World War II. The emplacement of the carriage and howitzer from their trailers required the assistance of a 20-ton Loraine Crane M2, which was part of the table of organization of these battalions. The crane was accompanied by a clamshell bucket attachment on a trailer behind, which was used to help dig an associated firing pit. It took about two hours to emplace the howitzers. On the other hand, the 240mm howitzer was also the most powerful weapon deployed by US artillery units during the war, able to fire a 360lb (165kg) projectile 25,225 yards (23km).

Wheeled transport wagons proved to be inadequate when moving the 240mm howitzer over soft soil, owing to the weight of the weapon's components. In May 1943, development continued on potential improvements, including wider tires or a tracked suspension. The modified M1E1 carriage was moved using a T17E1 transport wagon with a pair of tracked suspension limbers. The wheeled M2 transport wagon was replaced with the T16E1 cannon transport wagon, which had a set of three medium tank bogies on either side. In June 1944, the Army Ground Forces requested that a single battalion with six howitzers on the new tracked transport wagons be deployed to the southwest Pacific and this unit used the pilot equipment. After training in Hawaii and New Caledonia, the battalion saw combat in the fighting for Manila.

As mentioned earlier, the 240mm howitzer was designed alongside an 8-in. gun version that shared a related carriage. The main advantage of the 8-in. gun over the 240mm howitzer was greater range: 33,635 yards (30.7km) vs. 22,225 yards (20.3km), though at the expense of a lighter 240lb (109kg) projectile. The 8-in. gun actually proved to be a more troublesome project than its howitzer twin because of problems with premature bore wear induced by the detonation of its massive 106lb (48kg) propellant charge. Excessive barrel erosion reduced the accuracy of the weapon. In spite of these problems, production started on the 8-in. gun alongside the 240mm howitzer in November 1942, even though it was not standardized as the 8-in. Gun M1 on Carriage M2 until January 1944.

The 8-in. gun and carriage had a number of differences from the similar 240mm howitzer in regard to the equilibrator and recoil system

The 8-in. gun and 240mm howitzer were so large that the carriage and cannon had to be transported separately and assembled in position. Here at Hesse, France, on November 17, 1944, a crane lowers an 8-in. gun assembly onto the carriage in Battery C, 243d Field Artillery Battalion. The cannon transport wagon is evident to the left. (NARA)

to accommodate the differences in the gun tube weight and recoil forces. As in the case of the 155mm gun and 8-in. howitzer, they could not simply swap barrels in the field. Despite this, the 8-in. gun was rushed into action in Italy to meet requests for a weapon capable of dealing with the long-range German 170mm gun. Four guns arrived in Italy in April 1944, two going to the Anzio front and two to Cassino. They proved enormously successful both in counter-battery fire against German long-range guns, and in long-range artillery missions.

There were numerous attempts to develop fixes for the barrel erosion, including rifling changes, chromium plating, and other techniques, none of which were standardized owing to the end of the war. As a result, production of the 8-in. gun totaled less than half of its 240mm howitzer twin, at only 139 guns by June 1945. Because of performance problems with the 8-in. gun tube, the 240mm howitzer version of this family was the predominant type in service. Some 21 240mm howitzer battalions were raised, with 15 serving in Europe and five in the Pacific, primarily in the Philippines in 1945. In contrast, only eight 8-in. gun battalions were formed, five serving in Europe and three in the Pacific, the latter mainly on the Philippines in 1945.

The most powerful US artillery weapon developed in World War II was the 914mm T1 "Little David" mortar, which could fire a 3,650lb (1,655kg) projectile some 9,000 yards (8.2km). Development started in March 1944, but it was not completed in time for deployment.

THE INTERNATIONAL DIMENSION

Foreign artillery in US service

Curiously enough, the first shot fired by US field artillery against the Wehrmacht in World War II came not from a US-manufactured howitzer, but from a British-manufactured 25-pdr. The 34th Division was the first US infantry division deployed to the ETO and at the time, its three 105mm battalions had not received their new howitzers. As a result, these battalions were equipped with British 25-pdrs during their training in Northern Ireland and Scotland in the spring of 1942. When deployed to Tunisia in November 1942, the division's 175th Field Artillery Battalion used its 25-pdrs in combat for the first time during the race for Tunis. The 34th Division's battalions were reequipped with the 105mm howitzer later in the Tunisian campaign after their 25-pdrs had been worn out.

So many German artillery pieces were captured in France in 1944 that a number of US field artillery battalions established "Z Batteries," which used the German weapons until the ammunition was exhausted. The only systematic use was by the US First Army's 32d Field Artillery Brigade, with two provisional battalions formed in the ETO in November 1944. So many German artillery weapons and shells had been captured in the summer fighting that it was decided temporarily to reorganize the battalion to exploit this windfall. Weapons used included German 105mm and 150mm field howitzers, 88mm antitank guns, and French 155mm guns.

In the Pacific theater, there was occasional use of Allied weapons. For example, during the Lae campaign on New Guinea, the 503d Parachute Infantry Regiment was assigned to drop on the mountainous Nadzab airstrip on September 5, 1943. With the paratroopers lacking any fire support, the Australian Army provided several "baby 25-pdrs," a lightweight version of the 25-pdr manufactured in Australia. These were air-dropped into Nadzab along with gunners of the 2/4th Field Regiment.

Following the heavy losses of US equipment in the Ardennes during the Battle of the Bulge, Britain loaned 100 25-pdrs and 300,000 rounds of ammunition to temporarily equip US field artillery battalions until

The 503d Parachute Infantry Regiment was supported by Australian "baby 25-pdrs" of the 2/4th Field Regiment during the airdrop on the Nadzab airstrip on September 5, 1943, in New Guinea, and are seen here several days after being used by US paratroopers. (NARA

The 244th Field Artillery Battalion was assigned the task of using up the ample supply of captured German artillery and ammunition. This is a captured German 88mm PaK 43/41 being used to support a 6th Armored Division operation during the Battle of the Bulge on December 21, 1944. (NARA)

additional supplies arrived from the United States. Many of these were used in battalions of the US Ninth Army, which at the time was attached to Montgomery's 21st Army Group.

International use

In comparison to other types of materiel such as tanks, aircraft, and trucks, US export of field artillery under the Lend-Lease program was very modest. The most significant recipients of Lend-Lease – Great Britain and the Soviet Union – were not very interested in US field artillery, since their artillery differed from US calibers. In the case of the British Army, the exception was in light artillery and heavy artillery. In addition, some Canadian-produced 25-pdrs, funded by the United States, were categorized as Lend-Lease aid even though not actually manufactured in the US.

The situation was quite different in the postwar years, when the US delivered a considerable amount of field artillery to allies around the world under the Military Assistance Program, and the Foreign Military Sales program. Indeed, types such as the 105mm Howitzer M2A1, redesignated as the 105mm Howitzer M101 after the war, are still in use around the world a half-century later.

US LEND-LEASE FIELD ARTILLERY DELIVERIES, 1941–45			
	UK	China	France	Latin America
75mm Gun M1916	170	–	–	2
75mm pack howitzer	826	637	68	60
75mm field howitzer	–	125	–	–
25-pdr	192	62	–	–
105mm Howitzer M2A1	16	476	239	223
105mm Howitzer M3	2	–	94	18
155mm howitzer	236	36	12	18
155mm GPF gun	54	–	48	2
155mm Gun M1A1	184	–	25	–
8-in. howitzer	610	–	–	–
8-in. gun	17	–	–	–
240mm howitzer	28	–	–	–

CANNON ON THE MOVE

Field artillery motorization

A major goal of the 1941 artillery modernization plans was the development of dedicated prime movers for towed field artillery. While smaller weapons such as the 75mm pack howitzer and 105mm howitzer could be towed by trucks, the larger weapons posed a problem, particularly when being towed over rough terrain. As a result, several HSTs were developed for this role. As in the case of the artillery, the Army had an extensive program to develop prime movers prior to the war, but insufficient funds for a transition to series production. Due to space considerations, the account here is limited to those types that actually entered serial production, but a number of other types were developed during the war.

The M4 18-ton HST was developed by the Allis-Chalmers Co. and was intended for the 3-in. and 90mm guns, the 155mm gun, and 8-in. howitzer. The T9E1 pilot entered trials in late 1942, and the tractor used some M4 medium tank suspension components such as track, road-wheels, and drive sprocket. It was accepted for production in 1943 and could be configured with different ammunition boxes depending upon the type of weapon being towed. The two most common configurations were the Class A for the 90mm antiaircraft gun (54 rounds) and the Class B for the 155mm gun (30 rounds) and 8-in. howitzer (20 rounds). The final production run of 259 vehicles was in the M4A1 configuration, which had the bogies spaced out from the hull to permit the use of extended end connectors on the tracks for better flotation in soft soil. Many 155mm gun and 8-in. howitzer battalions in the ETO were equipped with this vehicle, though some units retained heavy trucks such as the Mack NO.

The M5 13-ton HST was developed by International Harvester Co. in 1942 on the basis of the earlier T13 medium tractor design. It used some suspension components from the M5 light tank, again such as the wheels, track, and drive-sprocket. The T21, prototype to the M5, underwent trials in 1942 and entered production in 1943. Although authorized for use with the 105mm howitzer, it was more commonly used in 4.5-in. gun and 155mm howitzer battalions. Ammunition was carried in a special rear compartment and it could carry 38 rounds of 4.5-in. or 24 rounds of 155mm ammunition. There were complaints from the field that the tractor lacked a self-defense weapon, and in February 1944 the Ordnance

Department approved the addition of a M49C ring mount for the .50-cal. heavy machine gun over the troop compartment. This was in some cases modified in the field or at depots using kits, and was eventually incorporated at the production plant. The final production batch of 589 tractors was built in the M5A1 configuration, which had a full width cab front reminiscent of the M4 HST and a permanent roof instead of the canvas type used earlier.

Development of the M6 38-ton HST was started in February 1942 by Allis-Chalmers. The T23 pilot vehicle resembled a scaled-up version of the firm's M4 HST, though it was substantially larger. Although standardized in June 1943, production did not begin until 1944. These delays forced the Army to field expedient prime movers until the M6 HST became available. The first of these was the M33 prime mover, which was converted from surplus M31 tank-recovery vehicles (TRVs). This was based on the M3 medium tank, but had the recovery equipment, crane, and turret removed. It was deployed to the Italian theater with the first 240mm howitzer battalions in the spring of 1944.

A shortage of surplus M31 TRVs led to the decision to convert M32B1 TRVs to the prime mover role as the M34 at the Chester Tank Depot. This program produced the shortest-lived of the three expedient prime movers, with only 24 built. A more practical conversion was the use of surplus M10A1 tank-destroyer hulls with the turret removed, designated as the M35 prime mover. These were converted at the Lima tank plant in 1944, and the M35 was the most common type deployed with 240mm howitzer battalions in France in 1944. The M6 HST finally arrived in the ETO in the spring of 1945 with a small number of heavy field artillery battalions, but it was a relatively rare type.

The M4 HST was the standard prime mover for the 155mm gun and 8-in. howitzer. This M4 is emplacing an 8-in. howitzer of the 999th Field Artillery Battalion (Colored) near Nantes-Gassicourt, France, on August 20, 1944. This was one of a number of segregated African-American artillery units serving in the ETO in 1944–45. (NARA)

FIELD ARTILLERY PRIME MOVER PRODUCTION, 1941–45

	1943	1944	1945	Total
M4 HST	1,644	2,911	1,256	5,811
M5 HST	975	3,503	1,401	5,879
M6 HST	0	724	511	1,235
M33 PM*	60	49	0	109
M34 PM*	0	24	0	24
M35 PM*	0	209	0	209
Total	2,679	7,420	3,168	13,267

*Prime mover conversions

Field artillery mechanization

The Westervelt Board had recommended the widespread mechanization of artillery when funds permitted, that is, mounting the artillery on self-propelled tracked vehicles. Although there was a good deal of experimentation with self-propelled artillery in the early 1920s, this mode of deployment was very controversial and generally rejected through the interwar years. Artillery officers felt that the existing tractors were simply too slow and unreliable, and preferred motorization to mechanization.

The M33 prime mover was used as an expedient vehicle until the arrival of the M6 HST, and one is seen here towing a 240mm cannon transport wagon near Mt. Porchia, Italy, on January 27, 1944. These were most commonly seen with the three heavy artillery battalions in Italy in early 1944. (NARA)

Attitudes towards mechanization changed after 1940, largely due to the formation of the US Armored Force. The tank officers wanted artillery weapons that could keep pace with the tank units. As an expedient, the 105mm howitzer was mounted on the M3 half-track as the T19 105mm HMC, and 324 were manufactured by the Diamond T Car Company from January to April 1942. This was used by the first armored field artillery battalions in Tunisia in 1942–43, but also was used by infantry cannon companies pending the arrival of the M3 105mm howitzer. The T19 was not an entirely satisfactory design, and in the meantime, the Ordnance Department adapted the 105mm Howitzer M2A1 to the M3 medium tank chassis as the M7 105mm HMC; by the time it entered production the M4 medium tank was being built, so the M7 is usually considered a variant of the M4 (Sherman) medium tank. The M7 became the only significant self-propelled artillery weapon of the US field artillery in World War II. Production of the M7 began at the American Locomotive Co. in April 1942 and continued, with several interruptions, through October 1944, with some 3,314 M7s being completed. Since the M4A3 medium tank was selected by the Army in the summer of 1943 as its preferred variant, in 1944 production shifted to a version based on this chassis, the M7B1, and it was manufactured at the Pressed Steel Car Co. from March 1944 to February 1945, with 826 built, bringing the grand total of M7 wartime production to 4,140 vehicles.

The M7 first entered combat during the campaign on Sicily in July 1943 with the armored field artillery battalions of the 2d Armored Division. As in the case of the T19, some were also deployed with infantry cannon companies, but this became less common in Europe by the end of 1943 as the new M3 105mm howitzer became the authorized weapon under the revised September 1943 organization table. Another secondary use for the M7 was as an expedient assault gun in the headquarters companies of tank battalions until the new M4 105mm assault gun became available. Assault guns were the artillery weapons assigned to armored and cavalry units for direct-fire support and were manned by armored force or cavalry troops, not field artillery troops.

The M35 prime mover was a turretless M10 tank destroyer and was used to tow the components of super-heavy artillery. Here one is seen towing an 8-in. gun on its cannon transport wagon. (NARA)

During 1943, the Army decided to extend the use of the M7 105mm HMC beyond the armored divisions and to raise armored field artillery battalions that could be assigned for corps support. In total, some 67 armored field artillery battalions were equipped with the M7; 62 served in the European campaigns (48 divisional, 14 non-divisional) and three battalions served in the Pacific, all non-divisional corps-support battalions that fought in the Philippines. The US Marine Corps began acquiring the M7B1 105mm HMC in 1944 to replace the old M3 75mm Gun Motor Carriage (GMC) in their Special Weapons Battalion. These were employed as direct-fire assault guns and saw combat in the final campaigns of 1945, such as on Okinawa. The M7 was also widely used in US Army infantry cannon companies in the final campaigns of 1944–45 in the Pacific, even though the towed M3 105mm howitzer was preferred in the ETO.

The US Army adopted another 105mm howitzer vehicle during the war, but not as a field artillery weapon. The Armored Force wanted a medium tank fitted with a 105mm howitzer to serve as an assault gun, and this was manufactured on both the M4 and M4A3 chassis. As in the case of other assault guns such as the M8 75mm HMC, these weapons were manned by tankers and not field artillery troops.

One of the most controversial, yet successful, self-propelled guns of the war was the M12 155mm GMC. This Ordnance Department scheme vehicle combined the venerable 155mm GPF on an M3 medium tank chassis. A total of 100 were built from September 1942 to March 1943, along with 100 of the associated M30 cargo carriers for ammunition. The artillery branch had little interest in them as they were not well suited to the usual corps-support roles, due to the limited elevation of their guns. They attracted more attention from US Army officers in Europe, who were convinced that they would be valuable for cracking open heavy bunkers during the assault on the Siegfried Line. As a result, in February 1944, 75 were reconditioned with new M4 tank components and issued to five armored field artillery battalions earmarked for the ETO. There they saw extensive use along the Siegfried Line in fall 1944, and were enormously successful in this specialized mission, winning many accolades from the infantry units they supported.

A more versatile heavy self-propelled gun was in development in 1943–44 to carry the 155mm Gun M1A1 (T83) and 8-in. howitzer (T89). Based on a widened M4A3 tank chassis, a total of 394 M40 155mm GMCs

The principal US self-propelled field artillery vehicle of World War II was the M7 105mm HMC, which combined the durable M4 medium tank chassis with the M2A1 105mm howitzer. (NARA)

were built, production beginning in February 1945, as well as 48 of the similar M43 8-in. HMC later in 1945. Although the series production vehicles arrived too late to see combat, a pilot T83 and a T89 were rushed to Germany in February 1945 as part of the Zebra mission to test new equipment. Both were configured with the 155mm gun and saw combat in the final months of the war alongside the M12 155mm GMC in the 991st Field Artillery Battalion.

Two other new self-propelled guns entered production too late to see combat, the M37 105mm HMC and the M41 155mm HMC. Both were based on the new M24 tank chassis and did not see combat until the Korean conflict began in 1950. Self-propelled artillery proved so successful in World War II that the postwar Committee on Organization recommended that the US Army abandon towed artillery altogether in favor of self-propelled guns.

Infantry cannon companies used the T19 105mm HMC in 1942–43 in North Africa and the early stages of the Italian campaign. This T19 is seen in Tunisia in 1943. (NARA)

US MECHANIZED FIELD ARTILLERY PRODUCTION, 1941–45					
	1942	1943	1944	1945	Total
T19 105mm HMC	324	–	–	–	324
M7 105mm HMC	2,028	786	500	176	3,490
M7B1 105mm HMC	–	–	664	162	826
M37 105mm HMC	–	–	–	150	150
M12 155mm GMC	60	40	–	–	100
M41 155mm HMC	–	–	–	85	85
M40 155mm GMC	–	–	–	394	394
M43 8-in. HMC	–	–	–	48	48
Total	2,412	826	1,164	1,015	5,417

FURTHER READING

US artillery of World War II has not attracted the amount of attention of other weapons, such as tanks, infantry weapons, aircraft, and warships, and there are very few specialized studies. Sad to say, there is nothing in print comparable to the excellent Crowell report of 1919 that detailed US artillery development and production in World War I. Ian Hogg's *British & American Artillery of World War II* (Arms & Armour: 1978) remains the best broad survey of the technical aspects of wartime US artillery, but was based primarily on the technical manuals, and is unreliable when discussing deployment. Self-propelled guns have received considerably more attention than the towed weapons, and Richard Hunnicutt's series of books on US tank development are an excellent resource. My own photo history in the Concord "Armor at War" series provides the most thorough pictorial account of self-propelled artillery in combat during the war.

The Ordnance Department prepared some histories of artillery development programs after the war which were never published, and these are scattered in Record Group 156 at the US National Archives and Records Administration II (NARA) at College Park, Maryland, and other facilities such as the US Army Ordnance Museum at Aberdeen Proving Ground, Maryland. The three histories of the Ordnance Department in the US Army "Green Book" World War II history series mentioned below put the development of artillery in the broader perspective of US Army programs during the war, but have few details on development. The TRADOC field artillery history provides a useful summary of the development of artillery organization and doctrine, especially in

The M12 155mm GMC was built in modest numbers but proved to be a highly successful direct-fire weapon for attacking the fortified Siegfried Line. This one, nicknamed "Buccaneer," is seen in action along the French frontier on November 25, 1944. (NARA)

the prewar years. A number of masters theses have been prepared over the years at the US Army Command and General Staff College at Fort Leavenworth dealing with wartime artillery developments, such as Scott McMeen's "Field Artillery Doctrine Development 1917–1945" (1991). The production data presented here was summarized from the War Production Board's 1947 internal publication, "Official Munitions Production of the United States," from the copy located at the US Army Military History Institute (MHI), Carlisle Barracks, Pennsylvania.

For those interested in more details on the wartime weapons, the US Army Ordnance technical manuals (TM9-) provide a good deal of data, and further information on operating the weapons can be found in the field manuals (FM). These manuals are available at many US archives such as MHI, some are available on-line from the MHI website, and some are available in digital form from CD publishers.

Other titles worth viewing are:

Comparato, Frank, *Age of the Great Guns* (Stackpole: 1965)

Crowell, Benedict, *America's Munitions 1917–1918* (GPO: 1919)

Dastrup, Boyd, *King of Battle: A Branch History of the US Army's Field Artillery* (US Army TRADOC: 1991)

Green, Constance, *et al.*, *The Ordnance Department: Planning Munitions for War* (GPO: 1955)

Hogg, Ian, *The American Arsenal* (reprint of 1944 Catalog of Standard Ordnance Items); (Greenhill: 1996)

Mayo, Lida, *The Ordnance Department: On Beachhead and Battlefront* (GPO: 1968)

Schreier, Konrad, *Standard Guide to US World War II Tanks and Artillery* (Krause: 1994)

Thomson, Harry, and Lida Mayo, *The Ordnance Department: Procurement and Supply* (GPO: 1960)

Zaloga, Steven J., *US Armored Artillery in World War II* (Concord: 2002)

Two pilot systems for the new T83 155mm SPG and T89 8-in. HMC were sent to the ETO in February 1945 for combat trials, but both were configured with the 155mm Gun M1A1. They served in combat during the final months of the war, and here one is seen in action in Germany on March 30, 1945, with the wreckage of a Ju-87 Stuka dive-bomber in the foreground. (NARA)

COLOR PLATE COMMENTARY

ARMY ARTILLERY MODELS AND MARKINGS

US field artillery was uniformly painted in overall lusterless olive drab. Although a number of engineering publications recommended various types of camouflage painting, these were exceedingly uncommon as they were regarded as a waste of time. The preferred method of camouflage was the use of camouflage nets over the gun positions. There were some exceptions, such as the use of whitewash during the winter of 1944–45. Field artillery usually carried no unit markings or any other sort of tactical marking.

A: THE PREWAR LEGACY
A: 75mm Pack Howitzer M1A1 on Carriage M1

The 75mm pack howitzer was originally mounted on a box-trail carriage with wooden-spoked wheels. This configuration was rarely used by the US Army except in difficult terrain conditions where mule or horse transport was necessary, such as the Burma theater.

2: 155mm Howitzer M1917A1 on Carriage M1918A1

The Schneider was in service in the US Army in both French-manufactured versions, such as the one here, and the US-manufactured M1918. The motorization program of the mid-1930s resulted in the addition of pneumatic tires as well as some other small detail changes such as hand-brakes to lock the wheels.

3: 155mm Gun M1918M1 on Carriage M3

The 155mm Gun M1918M1 was high-speed in 1941 for motorized traction. This weapon was used in limited numbers in the early Pacific campaigns, such as in the Philippines and Guadalcanal, but seldom afterwards.

B: 105MM HOWITZER M2A1 ON CARRIAGE M2A2

This was the final configuration of the M2A1 howitzer during the war, using the M2A2 carriage with its distinctive auxiliary splinter shield on the front. The exceptions to the overall olive-drab paint finish are evident here: the cleaning stakes on the left trails were sometimes left in varnished wood finish, and the aiming stakes on the right trails are in the usual divided white/red pattern.

C: 105MM HOWITZER M3 ON CARRIAGE M3A1

The 105mm Howitzer M3 used a lightweight carriage and so had to be lowered to the ground to create a stable firing platform. The sighting instruments were carried in a small

The British 21st Army Group loaned the US 12th Army group some 100 25-pdr field guns to temporarily make up for losses during the Battle of the Bulge. Here a battery from the 76th Field Artillery Battalion is seen supporting the 2d Infantry Division near Schoneseiffen on February 3, 1945. (NARA)

box strapped to the trails during transport. Although the weapon fired the same projectiles as the larger M2A1 105mm howitzer, it had to use less powerful propelling charges due to the limits of its carriage. As a result, the ammunition for the M3 was painted differently, with a solid yellow high-explosive projectile instead of the more common olive-drab projectile with yellow markings.

D: 105MM HOWITZER M2A1 ON CARRIAGE M2

This plate shows the initial production version of the 105mm Howitzer M2A1 with the M2 carriage. The carriage is distinguishable by the battery box on the right trail that was used with the Warner electric brakes. The later M2A1 carriage deleted this feature, though some M2 carriages were altered to this standard by leaving the box in place but removing the battery, wiring, and brakes.

The M6 HST was the preferred prime mover for super-heavy artillery, but was not deployed until late 1944. This M6 is towing a tracked T17E1 carriage transport wagon for the 240mm howitzer in Hawaii, on December 28, 1944. (NARA)

The 105mm howitzer's ammunition generally came packaged in one of three fashions: a two-round wooden box, a four-round wooden box, or a one-round metal tube. Within these containers, the ammunition was packaged in a black fiber-board tube with colored tape to identify the type – yellow in the case of high explosive. The 105mm ammunition was semi-fixed, that is, it came packaged with the propellant casing separate from the round to allow the gunner to select the number of increments in the bag charge for the necessary range, deleting however many to reach the right number. Once this was done, the propellant was placed inside the brass casing, and the casing joined to the projectile, so when loaded, the round was a single piece. The projectile color helped identify the type: olive drab with yellow markings for high explosive and HEAT (High-Explosive Anti-tank), gray with yellow markings for smoke.

E: 155MM HOWITZER M1 ON CARRIAGE M1
The 155mm Howitzer M1 used a split trail M1 carriage with a folding base-plate at the front to provide a very stable three-point suspension when firing. During transit, the square base-plate was stowed on top of the trails, while the recoil spades were removed and stowed on the outside of the trails.

Like most heavy field artillery pieces, the M1 howitzer used separated ammunition. The propellant came in an acrylic cotton cloth bag charge consisting of the base charge, which was always fired, plus a number of smaller increments that varied in number depending on the range to target. Before loading the bag charge, the gunner would remove any necessary increments to arrive at the proper propellant load. On heavy field artillery, two types of propellant charges were supplied, "Green bag" charges that contained less propellant and were intended for targets in the inner zones of fire, and "White bag" charges for targets in the outer zone. These were distinguished by the color of the cloth bag liners. Heavy artillery projectiles came with an inert plug in the fuse pocket at the front with a ring for ease of handling. Prior to firing, the gunner would unscrew the plug and replace it with the appropriate fuse.

F 155MM GM1A ON CARRIAGE M1
Due to its enormous recoil, the 155mm Gun M1A1 was lowered to the ground before firing. To further reduce the effect of recoil, the M1 carriage was fitted with two sets of recoil spades, one set behind the wheels and one set at the rear of the split trails. The top illustration shows it in travel mode with the M2 heavy carriage limber in place and the barrel locked in position, while the lower side view shows the gun in firing position with the trails extended, the wheels raised, and the recoil spades in position.

G 240MM HOWITZER M1 ON CARRIAGE M1 (TRANSPORT MODE)
The enormous size of the 240mm Howitzer M1 made it difficult to transport and emplace. The first production series used wheeled transport wagons to carry the howitzer, the M2A1 cannon transport wagon (1) to carry the cannon and recoil system, and the M3 carriage transport wagon (2). Some of the battalions deployed in the Pacific used an improved system with tracked wagons – the T16E1 cannon transport wagon (3) and the T17E1 carriage transport wagon (4). The cannon could be assembled on the carriage by two methods, using a crane for speed or using a winch if the crane was not available.

The gun crew of a 155mm Gun M1A1 ram home the projectile while the gunner to the left holds the propellant bag charge during the fighting in the Ardennes in January 1945. (NARA)

INDEX